The Antichrist
…the one who opposes what is good in the world…

SEMISI PONE

Copyright © Rainbow Enterprises Books

Publisher: Rainbow Enterprises Books

ISBN: 978-1-98-851138-2

All rights reserved. No part of this book shall be reproduced, in any way, without prior written permission from the writer and copyright holder.

> Note. As in many other books by the same author, quotes are taken directly from Wikipedia rather than individual writers to promote this excellent work. The author supports the Wikipedia encyclopedia which promote excellence in education.

CONTENT

Introduction

Chapter 1....What the Bible say about the Antichrist..................1

Chapter 2....The New Zealand Parliament's decision...30

Chapter 3....The Signs of the Antichrist..................35

Chapter 4....What do other religions say about the Antichrist?....42

Introduction

In this book, I will discuss the **Antichrist** or what I call **Negative Energy** as a separate entity from **Satan** or the **Devil**. In my view, and according to the information I have gathered, the Antichrist is a separate entity although it is frequently referred to as Satan or the Devil. This proposal has been developed in my books GOD IS ENERGY. DO YOU BELIEVE?. According to the Christian Bible, Satan or the Devil is a fallen Angel with power to influence the Spiritual and Physical world. From all accounts, Angels are messengers and agents of God with tremendous power of a spiritual and physical nature. They could be interpreted as manifestations of God's power.

The Antichrist, however, is the polar opposite or negative energy that opposes the Christ or divine gift of God as enshrined in God the son according to the Trinity Concept. The idea of this book is to contribute to our understanding of what the apostles and Christian writers mean when they talk about the Antichrist.

It is important for mankind to understand this foundation of the Christian faith because it is what our world is build upon. Christians, and Christian believers, make up 60% or more of the world population. They control most of the finance, wealth, military arms and power of the world. Every Western and Eastern Christian Nation had based its laws, constitutions and values on the teachings of Jesus Christ and the Christian Bible.

Even though some Christian Nations, like New Zealand, is turning its back on Christianity and Jesus Christ, **New Zealanders cannot deny their values of love, tolerance, charity and forgiveness are based on the teachings of Jesus Christ,** yet the Parliament of New Zealand had removed Jesus Christ from its prayer.

Soon about a year after, 50 people were shot and killed in Christchurch and 39 were injured. It is the most horrendous and scariest massacre, destruction and disrespect for human life ever in New Zealand's existence.

It reminds me of what Pope Benedict XVI said in 2012;

'Violence is the tool of the Antichrist'

The question we must ask is this. Did the action of New Zealand's Parliament invite the Antichrist to take over power in New Zealand?

It has prompted me to write this book because I think we should start a modern conversation about this ancient foe.

Our Members of Parliament in New Zealand, and the public in general, should make themselves familiar with their ancestor's Christian faith. If we remove Jesus Christ, the light of the Christian world then the Antichrist will take over.

The power of darkness will rule over
New Zealand.

Only destruction and fear will result from
the negative energy that will pervade
every human, animal and available space
in the country.

Chapter 1....

What the Bible say about the Antichrist

The bible refers to the Antichrist in the book of John.

In John's first epistle chapter 4 verse 2 he says, **'By this you know the Spirit of God: every spirit that confesses that Jesus Christ has come in the flesh is from God, and every spirit that does not confess Jesus is not from God. And this is the spirit of the Antichrist, of which you have heard that it is coming; and now it is already in the world'.**

John also pointed out in chapter 2 verse 22, **'Who is the liar but the one who denies that Jesus is the Christ? This is the Antichrist, the one who denies the Father and the Son',** New Revised Standard Version (NRSV, 1989).

There are many others who have spoken out or written about the Antichrist.

Among them is **Pope Benedict XVI who said in the Sunday Angelus of March 11, 2012 that;**

'violence is the tool of the Antichrist'.

…Negative Energy…

I wish to discuss my personal experience of what I describe as 'negative energy' or 'evil spirits' in common Christian description. What I am pointing out is that, it is a very common phenomenon but we do not notice it or think of it consciously.

Let's look at some cases of seemingly normal 'accidents' or out of the ordinary happenings. **Odd happenings that really make me wonder.**

Case 1....Unusual happenings

I was doing some work watering a garden with a long hose. The lawn had plenty of space but as I moved along the hose got caught in a break in the footpath in the middle of the lawn. The chances of it getting caught in that small space is pretty remote in my view. I think of it as a 'mischievous spirit or negative energy' that gets in the way of my work. Most people will never think of it that way.

Case 2....Forceful spirits

I was loading some timber into my car and somehow one of the pieces seem to be forced towards the right rear light breaking it. I felt it like a 'wind' that pushes the heavy piece of timber towards the light casing causing it to break. Is it the negative spirit or something else trying to tell me something?

Case 3....Evil spirits

A Methodist Minister was talking about this type of negative energy in a sermon I attended as an 11 year old. He said that he was working in his garden weeding it with a hoe. Bits of sticks that he disturb with his hoe, which he pushes along on a long handle, to remove the weeds, repeated flew and hit him in the face. It was a distance of about 2 metres. The Minister said he recognized it is unusual and can only mean one thing. He was a famous spiritual healer, in our part of the world, and very often he comes across evil spirits in his work. He commanded the evil spirit to leave and continued his gardening work. Amazingly, he said, the flying pieces of sticks ceased to fly and hit him in the face.

I did not pay much attention to his story, but increasingly I am noticing many unusual happenings in my life as I began researching and writing about the Bible and Spiritual development.

I now think about the Methodist Minister and his stories, during that sermon in our little church 47 years ago, and he was talking about evil spirits that try to stop him from doing the work of God.

I read and write a lot of books and blogs about Christianity in the 21st century and beyond and I feel that the little accidents the Methodist Minister was taking about is happening to me too! I am becoming 'more aware and sensitive' about my surroundings.

Case 4....The Evil One

I have talked about this before. When I started writing my first book of the series GOD IS ENERGY. DO YOU BELIEVE? a few years ago, our computer at home broke down. I went and continued my work on the local library computer. I returned home to watch the 12 pm news and make some sandwiches for lunch. While preparing lunch, the loudest clap of thunder I have heard, in my whole life, rocked our house for several seconds. I thought it was an earthquake. It sounded to me like GODZILLA, the monster in the movie. It sounded as if the monster lizard was roaring in our living room where I was! It was very, very scary. I was the only one at home. It really shook me.

It started raining a few minutes after with thunder in the distance. I thought to myself, what is the chance that the thunder can do that? Can the thunder sound like Godzilla and rock the house? Is somebody angry that I am writing a book about God? Why did our computer break down?

...Conclusion...

I think you will agree that these cases are unusual. They are not just 'everyday happenings'. Most people will just dismiss them as 'nothing' because they do not have the background knowledge to recognize them for what they are.

If you extrapolate these phenomena you will begin to understand that 'things' do not happen by accident or just **random events.**

…A test for randomness…

When I was doing my Master of Science degree, part of my research work was to analyze how a virus disease spreads in a plantation of vanilla plants on the islands of Tongatapu and Vava'u in the Kingdom of Tonga. The virus causes dieback of the vines and death of the plants in a matter of a few weeks after symptoms appear. First, I analyzed how it spreads along the rows of vanilla plants and also how it spreads across rows of plants. The statistical analysis I used will determine whether the virus spread is **a random event or whether it is a 'cluster'**.

If it is random then it is just a natural occurrence….but if it is a cluster, then there is a vector or 'something' spreading the virus to cause the disease. It turned out the diseased plants were clustered and the vector was a large number of aphids populating weeds inside the plantation, spreading the virus across the rows of vanilla plants. Growers were also implicated as spreading the virus along the rows of vanilla plants. A person who is just looking at the diseased plants will never understand how the virus spreads. The test for randomness using complicated statistical inferences and calculations enabled me to understand what is happening.

In statistical language, after the analysis, when the significance level is high at 95% or more (99%) then you are very confident that the spread of the virus is **not just random but caused by 'something'**. In the case of vanilla in Tonga, an insect called an aphid carry the virus on its proboscis or feeding tube from infected vanilla plants to healthy vanilla plants. The growers themselves carry the virus on the vanilla sap, on their tools and hands, from infected to healthy vanilla plants. These two events causes the virus to cause disease in 'clusters' of plants giving away the mode of spread.

In the realm of faith, God and spirituality, we can use evidence from those whose experience and words we trust. It is our 'test for randomness' to enable us to make decisions concerning the spirit world. Because in the spirit world it is the affairs of the spirit that matters. The human body in that sense is just a heap of dirt on the earth.

…Why do we have power over the 'Devil'…

Do we have a test to analyze the events attributed to evil spirits? Or are they just random events? Are we confident, at the 95% or 99% levels, when we conclude that bits of sticks that fly and hit us in the face is not a random event but caused by 'something'?

Here's the proof;

When the Methodist Minister commanded the evil spirit to leave, the

flying bits of sticks ceased and he was left in peace.

The Methodist Minister says that he would always 'rebuke' the evil spirits and send it 'back to hell' where it came from.

In John's first epistle Chapter 4 verse 4, New Living Translation (NLT) the apostle points out;

'But you belong to God, my dear children. You have already won a victory over those people, because the Spirit who lives in you is greater than the spirit who lives in the world.'.

I believe what John is referring here to the negative energy. The opposing force. The evil spirit. The one who is 'in the world'. Sometimes referred to as Satan or the Devil.

This topic is discussed, and developed, in my other books GOD IS ENERGY. DO YOU BELIEVE? Books 1-5.

…What does other religions say about the Negative Energy?…

The concept of Karma in Hinduism refers to;

'every action will have an opposite reaction'…

It means, in the spiritual world actions will manifest itself in the physical world. Very much like the Third Law of Motion by Sir Isaac Newton.

'For every action, there is an equal and opposite reaction'.

I have discussed this idea and relationships in GOD IS ENERGY. DO YOU BELIEVE? Book 1.

What the Methodist Minister, mentioned previously in this chapter, was referring to when he banished the 'negative energy' to leave immediately is the same power that John is talking about in his first epistle chapter 4 verse 4. **Although**

the negative energy or evil spirit (of the Antichrist) is strong, the one who is within us, or Jesus Christ, is stronger and we can reject the evil spirit and command it to leave. In other words, Christ, the Holy Spirit, is stronger. The Methodist Minister knew that Christ within him is stronger than the one throwing sticks at his face.

The concept of Karma is also known in Christianity. For example, the 10 commandments where God forbid 'his people' from worshiping other Gods for he will punish them **and their descendants.** Karma is also said to work through generations or reincarnations.

It is also implied in many of the teachings of Jesus Christ. For example, the **'sermon on the mount'** (Matthew Chapters 5, 6, 7) where an **event or human deed/virtue is followed by a blessing just like an action initiates a reaction in karmic philosophy.**

Quote from Matthew 5:3-8

(i) Blessed are the poor in spirit for theirs is the Kingdom of Heaven
(ii) Blessed are they that mourn for they will be comforted
(iii) Blessed are the meek for they shall inherit the earth
(iv) Blessed are they which hunger and thirst after righteousness for they shall be filled
(v) Blessed are the merciful for they shall obtain mercy
(vi) Blessed are the pure in spirit for they shall see God

Unquote

(vii) and so on...

Karma works like that according to Hinduism. The sins that you commit now will produce afflictions on yourself or future generations. I once read a book about an American spiritual healer, and in many of his cases he advised his patients to read certain verses in the Christian Bible. The man was not a Christian. Effectively, what he said was **'the disease was caused by sins in the past'** and reading those bible verses will neutralize the negative energy produced. According to the book, it worked! Just reading the bible corrected the problems of those patients.

...How does Negative Energy work?...

I use the term Negative Energy to describe the forces opposing the Positive Energy. In my books GOD IS ENERGY. DO YOU BELIEVE? Books 1-5, I have developed, and proposed, the idea that God must be intelligent energy because;

(i) God is everywhere
(ii) God is all powerful
(iii) God is invisible
(iv) God can empower weak entities
(v) God is all knowing

The description that God is omniscient and omnipotent is often used in

Christianity. It does follow that in the concept of Karma and Sir Isaac Newton's Third Law of Motion, we can safely conclude that if God is omniscient and omnipotent then the opposite is also as powerful.

We have read in the Christian Bible about the power of Jesus Christ because he is God the Son. The Antichrist, to use the Karma and Sir Isaac Newton's explanations, is just as powerful. I believe, this is why the Antichrist does affect our world. The Antichrist is also powerful like God.

Man's only saving grace is what John referred to;

'the one inside you is stronger than the one out there'

It follows logically, that if we allow the Antichrist to take over, if we are permissive and weak then it will rule our world. **The one out there will be stronger than you.** Mankind must understand this, it will be detrimental to the welfare of the human community.

In my view, the apostle John was talking about the Antichrist as a **'concentration of demonic energy opposed to positive energy (God)'.**

Therefore, the Antichrist is not a man of flesh and blood. It is the polar but opposite image of God. It is omniscient and omnipotent….only if we allow it to.

I have read some literature about demon worship or Satanic Worship. It is claimed that the Priests of the Devil also possess power like those of the Christian Churches.

The Ministers or Priest of the Christian Churches can perform these miracles according to historical accounts;

(i) Banish evil spirits in cases of demonic possession
(ii) Influence the physical world through prayer

(iii) Heal the sick through prayer

Apparently, Demonic Priests or Devil Worshipers also claim the same powers!

If the Christian Ministers and followers of Jesus Christ can perform miracles in his name, then it logically follows that the followers of the opposite (Antichrist) can do the same. This is how the negative energy works. It is a reflection of the positive energy, with the same power.

…Manifestations of the Antichrist…

To put this in perspective, we can read about what others say, like Pope Benedict XVI. He says, in 2012, that **'violence is the tool of the Antichrist'.**

This violence can take on many forms.

From small incidences in your life, like the small sticks flying up and hitting the Methodist Minister in the face, clumsy and awkward situations that cause problems in your everyday life, to huge accidents and violent events that rock the world and scare its inhabitants.

Why would I attribute these occurrences to the Antichrist? Isn't it the fault of the individuals themselves? Isn't that why we put those individuals in jail? Because they are responsible for the mass shootings and other violent happenings?

Let's look at the bigger picture from a spiritual point of view. I had discussed this in some detail in my books GOD IS ENERGY. DO YOU BELIEVE? Book 1.

Suppose you have a body with all its organs and parts intact and in good condition BUT it is a dead body. We ask the question. Why is it dead? Isn't all the parts and organs intact and good condition? Why can't it stand up and move like a good body

I think you will agree, there is something else that make it alive. It needs an injection of energy to revive it into life.

Just like they revive the dead people in the hospitals using electric energy.

It logically follows therefore, that if the body needs energy to live there must be intelligence in that energy. It must be a higher power that control that energy to give the human body life....otherwise why would energy give life? And revive the dead body? That is why I propose that God is that energy. A positive, friendly energy.

We can also conclude that if the energy is not friendly and it causes death and destruction then it is a negative energy. The Antichrist.

...God's Love...

God's love has always been man's salvation through grace. A divine gift.

The Gospel of John 3:16 tells us why.

'For God so loved the world that he gave his only son, that whoever

believeth in him shall never die but have eternal life.'

Killing other humans, destroying human resources and sabotaging human economic activity is not the work of a loving God. It is the work of the Antichrist.

Many people around the world often blame God for their misfortunes and blame God for the natural disasters but they do not understand how the spiritual world works and how it affects the physical world.

They must understand this.

Death, destruction and misery in the world is the work of the Antichrist.

The Christian Bible already pointed that out in the Gospels and Epistles of the New Testament written 2,000 years ago.

Pope Benedict XVI and other Christian writers also point that out. But why do humans not understand it or believe?

Why do humans prefer to remove Jesus Christ from their world, who is the preacher of love, forgiveness, tolerance and charity? And keep the Antichrist who is the killer and destroyer of all that is good in the world?

I can understand the logic of the New Zealand Parliament. They say that the prayer must be inclusive of all New Zealanders and reflect New Zealand's situation. That is, the New Zealand statistics suggest there are more non-Christians than Christians living in New Zealand.

It does point to one thing only. The Antichrist is in control of New Zealand's Parliament and Government. I can predict that we shall see more and more misery in New Zealand. More and more destruction and death in the future.

The apostle John also pointed out in chapter 2 verse 22, **'Who is the liar but the one who denies that Jesus is the Christ? This is the Antichrist, the one who denies the Father and the Son'**, New Revised Standard Version (NRSV, 1989).

The New Zealand Parliament has denied the Father and the Son by removing Jesus Christ from its prayer.

Understand this, in God's time a 1,000 years is just a moment. When Jesus predicted the fall of the Roman Empire and the Jewish Kingdom, it took hundreds of years before it actually happened.

The fall of New Zealand will also take time. It will not happen overnight but gradually the darkness will replace the light. Unless we heed the message in John's epistle chapter 4 verse 4.

'The one inside us is stronger than the one out there'.

The Holy Spirit is inside us. It is the one that give us life. That make the dead body move and think and do things. Without that energy, the body is just a piece of earth that will rot and return to its former state. A piece of dirt on the ground.

Where is the proof?

Isn't the dead raised with electric energy at the modern hospitals? That is proof that energy is the source of life. God.

...Science...

Science explains it by suggesting that it was evolution that brought about the gradual changes that made modern man. A trial by error and selection of the fittest to survive. Do you believe that once your ancestors were monkeys? The greatest among us, Kings, Queens, the richest people in the world all descendants of one monkey?.

I believe in divine evolution and not 'accidental' evolution. Just as we have power over our destiny so does the animals and plants have power over theirs. Isn't that survival of the fittest? The ones who can adapt? I have discussed this topic in GOD IS ENERGY. DO YOU BELIEVE?. Book 1.

Your thoughts, your words and your actions have the power to influence your destiny and those of your descendants. Just like God's commandments he gave to Moses. Just like karma as believed by 2 billion Hindus and Buddhists.

> Many Christian writers and preachers say that the Antichrist is a Christlike person with great power to perform miracles who will convince the world that he is the Messiah. He will rule the world just before the second coming of Jesus Christ. Christ returns and will kill and destroy the Antichrist according to Biblical accounts and prophecy, before judgement day. This same event is also predicted in Islam and discussed in the Baha'i faith.

…How does God work?…
This is the most important topic of our discussion. Why does God only care about Jews, Christians, Buddhists, Hindus or Muslims?

Does God only prefer one particular group, race or ethnicity over others?

I like to use the 'car example' to explain what I believe is happening.

There are many brands and models of cars, but they all belong to the CAR category. Just like there are many truck brands and models and we group them in the TRUCK category…and so on.

Similarly, in the human family there are many races and ethnic groups. The Holy Spirit, as described by Christians, can take over the bodies of these humans irrespective of what they become when they are born onto the world. Just like a driver will get into a car or truck, irrespective of brand and model and drive it.

A baby can be born into a Christian family, Muslim family, Hindu and Buddhist family and so on. The spirit that make the baby alive does not belong to any church group or religion. The spirit is part of the Cosmic Spirit or God.

The Hindus believe that our existence on the Earth is a punishment and we must strive to be good so that we can be accepted back into the Cosmic Spirit or God. When we die, if we have been good, our spirit return to God.

The Christians believe that Jesus Christ is the human manifestation of the Holy Spirit or God. The deeds and teachings of Jesus Christ is the proof that he is not a human but a God.

It does seem that all the four major religions of Christianity, Islam, Hinduism and Buddhism believe in the same thing but differ in the details…and like humans they will tend to quarrel over who is right and who is wrong. That has festered as wars over religious beliefs for a 1,000 years or more. The crusades, the religious conflicts in many countries and so on.

If God favored the Christians he would have given us a sign. From the evidence here's the proof;

1. The Christian countries dominate the world of commerce.
2. The Christian countries dominate world trade.
3. The Christian countries are the wealthiest on Earth.
4. The Christian countries are the most advanced in terms of arms and technology.
5. The Christian countries give billions of dollars, goods and services to poor non-Christian countries every year.
6. The Christian Doctors and Nurses work tirelessly to save and cure diseases of non-Christians.
7. The Christian Universities teach and upskill non-Christians.

8. The Christian countries accept non-Christian refugees.
9. The Christian countries accept and employ non-Christian labor.
10. The Christian countries help non-Christian countries to prevent wars and improve governance.

We can list all the good deeds that Christians and their countries do for non-Christians and it will fill many books. **It does seem that God favors Christians!**

We have heard there are still problems, around the world, with Non-Christians who are violent towards Christians.

However, it does not stop the Christian Community from extending the helping and loving hand of Jesus Christ to all who need his help. Christian and Non-Christian alike.

...What is the problem?...

Here's the problem with the Antichrist. If you are not a Christian, you can be a weapon of the Antichrist against the Christians. We have witnessed the atrocities of Non-Christians against the Christians in the last 2,000 years. I cannot emphasize that point enough.

But the Christians have always managed to dominate and win through the power of the Holy Spirit (1 John, 4:4). We are stronger than the Antichrist.

However, it does not make it any less evil….if we allow the Antichrist to dominate, it will ensure the annihilation of the Christians.

Chapter 2....

The New Zealand Parliament's decision

The decision of the New Zealand Parliament to remove Jesus Christ from its prayer is very important....and a sign that the Antichrist has taken over New Zealand's Parliament.

The New Zealand Parliament has denied God the Son, Jesus Christ, which the apostle John pointed out. It makes the New Zealand Parliament an agent of the Antichrist.

The New Zealand Parliament Speaker's Decision to remove the Queen and Jesus Christ from the prayer has been criticized by many people around New Zealand, especially Christians. For example, Deputy Prime Minister, Hon. Winston Peters did suggest there should have been more consultation. Hon. Peters was of the opinion that the Speaker should have consulted with others and also take advice.

Thousands of people have marched to Parliament in Wellington and demanded that Jesus Christ should be put back into its prayer….without success. It does mean one thing, **we have allowed the one out there to be stronger than us.**

Apparently, according to many reports in the media, there has been many consultations before and advice sought but the conclusion was to leave the prayer wording as it is.

The old prayer wording;

THE OLD PRAYER:

Almighty God,

Humbly acknowledging our need for Thy guidance in all things, and laying aside all private and personal interests, we beseech Thee to grant that we may conduct the affairs of this House and of our country to the glory of Thy holy name, the maintenance of true religion and justice, the honour of the Queen, and the public welfare, peace, and tranquility of New Zealand, through Jesus Christ our Lord.

Amen.

This is the new version. The Speaker is on record as saying that he had consulted many people and he thought the new version is more inclusive of all New Zealanders. Both the Queen and Jesus Christ were left out of the prayer.

THE NEW VERSION:

Almighty God, we give thanks for the blessings which have been bestowed on New Zealand.

Laying aside all personal interests, we pray for guidance in our deliberations, that we may conduct the affairs of this House with wisdom and humility, for the public welfare and peace of New Zealand.

Amen.

…What happened in Christchurch?…

The violence in Christchurch, killing 50 people and wounding 39 is a sign that the Antichrist is gaining in strength. New Zealand has never been affected by such terror before.

Now the terror continues. The ANZAC Day celebrations has been cut back in numbers and also in locations. There was a fall out with Turkey where dawn celebrations were to be held. The Turks, who are Muslims, did not like comments made by the Australians, who are Christians.

We will see more and more of this kind of 'terror effect' taking over our lives in New Zealand.

…What can we do about it?…

We should try and slow down the growth and strength of the Antichrist by joining hands in acknowledging Jesus Christ as our Lord and Savior which will help banish the Antichrist back to the depths of hell, as the Methodist Minister would put it.

The Christians in New Zealand must rally together and put Jesus Christ back where he belongs, as our Lord and Savior.

Chapter 3….

The Signs of the Antichrist

These are signs that the Antichrist is in charge according to Biblical evidence.

1. We deny that Jesus is the Christ as explained in John chapter 2 verse 22;

'Who is the liar but the one who denies that Jesus is the Christ? This is the Antichrist, the one who denies the Father and the Son'.

Note: This has happened in the New Zealand Parliament where the name of Jesus Christ has been removed from the Parliament prayer.

2. The appearance of false messiahs who will deceive the people/world. I believe this refers to anyone in authority who will mislead the people.

'For false messiahs and false prophets will appear and produce great signs and omens, to lead astray, if possible, even the elect'.

— Matthew 24:24 and Mark 13:22 NRSV (1989)

Most of the biblical references and other writings about the Antichrist, in the last 2,000 years, does not make much sense. The Pope and the Catholic Church were accused as the Antichrist. It was more a sign of the times and the overpowering rule of the Pope that many of the European believers repelled against it. Calling anyone the Antichrist was used as a weapon of rebellion, calling anyone that is unpopular the Antichrist. Pope John Paul II, for example, is just one of the accused.

It is my view that the original meaning of the Antichrist refers to the opposing forces against Jesus Christ. This is how the idea is being developed in this book using biblical evidence and personal experience that supports the apostle John's epistle that the Antichrist is the opposing force to Jesus Christ.

Many of the latter Christian writers refer to the Antichrist as the opposing forces to salvation through Christ and it is basically the work of Satan himself.
This includes the view of the 'Church of Jesus Christ of Latter Day Saints'.

…Martin Wight…

A devout Christian and political theorist Martin Wight writing immediately after World War Two, favoured the revival of the Antichrist doctrine; not as a person, but as a recurrent situation featuring **'demonic concentrations of power'**

Demonic concentration of power is an excellent description of what the apostle John was trying to say.

…The Demonic Power of the Antichrist…

It is the demonic power of the Antichrist which should have us worried. It is what the apostle was trying to point out. Every major religion know this, without God's power we can be overcome by the negative energy of demonic proportions which the apostle called the Antichrist.

…How and where can we find the Antichrist?…

The Antichrist, like God, is everywhere. Its power can influence our lives negatively.

Consider this about New Zealand.

1. The New Zealand Statistics show there are more Non-Christians than Christians in New Zealand.

The New Zealand Statistics also show that;

(i) There are more than 500,000 incidences of family violence in New Zealand that require Police attendance, every year.

(ii) There is a call to the Police every 5.5 minutes to report family violence in New Zealand. The media just announced last week that it is now every 4 minutes!

(iii) New Zealand has the highest rate of youth suicide in the developed world.

(iv) More than 20 men and women are killed every year in family violence incidences in New Zealand

Can you suggest why there is such a terrible, terrible violent affliction that affect family life in New Zealand?

Who do you think is responsible for all these violence and misery in so many New Zealand families?

Is it the drugs and alcohol?

Or is it something else? Something so evil and powerful that arose from the beginning with the light. It is the darkness. The powerful force that oppose all that is good in our world. The Antichrist.

We have removed Jesus Christ from our Parliament prayer. There are fewer Christians than Non-Christians in New Zealand. The situation is perfect for the Antichrist.

Some Christian writers refer to the Antichrist as the work of the Devil, Satan himself. The Evil One.

The apostle does give us hope. We do have the strong one within us. We can command the Evil One or the Antichrist to leave us and our families alone.

We can ask Jesus Christ to come back and save our communities from certain destruction. To save our children from the Evil One.

Chapter 4....

What do other religions say about the Antichrist?

The Antichrist is not only a Christian Idea only. Other religions too have also predicted the rise of the Antichrist. Here are some quotes from Wikipedia.

QUOTE....

Judaism

There are warnings against false prophets in the Hebrew Bible, but no personal anti-Messiah figure.

Islam

"The Deceiving Messiah" is an evil figure in Islamic eschatology. Although not mentioned in the Quran the details of his

coming and life is explicitly mentioned in the authentic hadith hence
Muslims believe he is to appear pretending to be the Messiah then God at a time in the future, before The Day of Resurrection, Judgement Day.

Jesus Christ (Isa) will defeat the Deceiving Messiah in the final days.

Ahmadi Muslim

Prophecies concerning the emergence of the Antichrist (*Al-Masīḥ ad-Dajjāl*) are interpreted in Ahmadiyya teachings as designating a specific group of nations centred upon falsehood instead of an individual, with the reference to the Antichrist as an individual indicating its unity as a class or system rather than its personal individuality. As such, Ahmadi Muslims identify the Antichrist collectively with the missionary expansion and colonial dominance of European Christianity throughout the world that was propelled by the Industrial Revolution. Mirza Ghulam Ahmad wrote extensively on this topic identifying the Antichrist principally with colonial missionaries who, according to him, were to be countered through argumentation rather than by physical warfare, and whose power and influence was to wane gradually. While the term *Dajjāl* is taken as a reference to the forces of falsehood in matters of ideology and religious belief, prophecies concerning Gog and Magog (or *Ya'jūj Ma'jūj*) are taken as relating to the duplicity in the realm of politics and the shattering of world peace by the same forces – whose ancestors are thought to be the Slavic and Teutonic peoples – and are seen as embodied by the political dominance of European powers. The conflict between Russia and the United States as two superpowers, or the militant rivalry between the communist and capitalist systems and their impact over the nations of the world, are thus seen as having occurred in accordance with prophecies concerning Gog and Magog. These powers cannot be defeated through military force and are to be overcome through prayer and divine intervention. Islam is then seen as that which alone would succeed in bringing people of different nations together as per the Quran.

> **Mirzā Ghulām Ahmad** (13 February 1835 – 26 May 1908) was an Indian religious leader and the founder of the Ahmadiyya Movement in Islam. He claimed to have been divinely appointed as the promised Messiah and Mahdi —which is the metaphorical second-coming of Jesus (*mathīl-i 'Isā*), in fulfillment of Islam's latter day prophecies, as well as the Mujaddid (centennial reviver) of the 14th Islamic century.

Baha'i

The Antichrist is considered to subvert the religion of God from the inner reality of man. "Christ was a divine Center of unity and love. Whenever discord prevails instead of unity, wherever hatred and antagonism take the place of love and spiritual fellowship, Antichrist reigns instead of Christ."

UNQUOTE....

It is very interesting that Ahmadi Muslims believe the Christians and Europeans to be the Antichrist. The recent migration of many Muslim refugees into Christian countries to escape the wars in the Middle East is probably an opportunity for those Muslims to start revolutions of prayer and ideology in Christian and European countries to oppose what they believe to be evil empires.

The rise of extremism in the Islam religion should be a huge concern to all European and Christian countries because, as we have seen in many violent events perpetuated by Muslims, it is a Holy War or Jihad in the eyes of Islam. The objective is to rid the world of those who do not share their beliefs. This is already well explained by many writers in Wikipedia and elsewhere. **Is it inspired by the Antichrist? We should discuss more of it and seek solutions in the spiritual and physical worlds.**

ABOUT THE AUTHOR

Semisi Pule also known as Semisi Pule Pone, Semisi Pone in short form, was born in the Kingdom of Tonga. He attended Longolongo Primary School and Tonga High School where he passed both his New Zealand School Certificate (1978) and University Entrance (1979) in 5 subjects. A rare achievement for Tongan education at the time.

He moved to New Zealand to further his studies at Mt Albert Grammar School (1980) then University of Auckland (1981) where he graduated with a Bachelor of Science in 1985.

He returned to Tonga and worked for the Ministry of Agriculture , Fisheries and Forests in June 1985 as an Agriculture Officer/Plant Pathologist . He carried out research on banana diseases and vanilla. He returned to Auckland University in 1987 to complete a Master of Science programme. He graduated with Honours in 1989.

He returned to Tonga and carried on his research work on vanilla, kava and squash viruses and was promoted to Senior Plant Virologist in 1991. His research results in Tonga is published in his book PLANT PROTECTION IN THE PACIFIC, books 1 and 2.

In March 1992, he joined the Institute for Research, Extension and training in Agriculture (IRETA) at the University of the South Pacific (USP), Alafua Campus as a Fellow in Tissue Culture. His research results at USP is published in his book PLANT PROTECTION IN THE PACIFIC 3.

In April 1993, he was appointed the Advisor and Co-ordinator of the South Pacific Commission (SPC) Plant Protection Service, Suva Campus, Fiji. The results of his work there are published in various reports and his book

PLANT PROTECTION IN THE PACIFIC.

He migrated with his family to New Zealand in June, 1996 where he was involved in various businesses.

He is now a writer with more than 200 books and ebooks in amazon.com, blurb.com and wheelers.co.nz

He also operates a small contracts business.

As a young child he was a frequent church goer and enjoyed church activities in the Methodist Church.

As a writer and publisher of many books and ebooks on Christian and others religion he is very interested in the effects of the Spiritual World on our lives in the Physical World. Many of his writings, readings and research on the topic reflect this. His series of books on GOD IS ENERGY. DO YOU BELIEVE? Discusses similar phenomena in

Christianity as well as what Science say or do which explains many of the Biblical truths.

www.ingramcontent.com/pod-product-compliance
Lightning Source LLC
Chambersburg PA
CBHW051703040426
42446CB00009B/1286